# Maximize YOUR Money: Golden Nuggets for the Home Refinance

Michael Baltazar

ISBN-13: 978-0692768662
ISBN-10: 0692768661

# DEDICATION

This book is dedicated to all my clients over the last eighteen years, who have trusted me with their homeownership dreams and goals. But especially to my amazing wife and awesome kids, who have supported my career and my many endeavors.

I love you all!

# Preface

Ladies and gentlemen, you have worked hard for your money. It doesn't matter if you are a millionaire or working your first real job. You showed up for work when you were expected to, put your time in and earned that paycheck. Believe it or not, that is the easy part. That is the most predictable part of your earnings. You show up and then you get paid. It's pretty simple, right?

What is not simple is how, when, where to spend that money. Now, this book is NOT about saving your Starbucks money and investing more in your 401k. This book is about how to Maximize YOUR Money when it comes to the mortgage on your home. Your mortgage may be the biggest loan you ever take out in your lifetime, so you want to make sure that you are not overpaying for it.

I want to share with you some of the golden nuggets to refinancing your home. When you are done reading this book, you will easily know whether or not refinancing is right for you. You may even find additional insight on ways that you can leverage a home refinance to put you and your family into a better economic position.

Again, the goal is to Maximize YOUR Money and have your investments make more sense for you.

Let's begin!

# Chapter 1: Breakeven ASAP!

Keep in mind that there are two "price tags" on every mortgage. There is the cost to "get the loan" and there is the cost to "have the loan." When the closing costs are low, the rate is going to be higher. When the rate is low, the costs are going to be higher. The goal should be to find the rate that saves you enough to recover your closing costs, within a reasonable time, to meet your goals. Let's look at a couple examples. Example #1: If you are saving $100 per month with your new loan and paid $4500 (for the new loan's closing costs) to get those savings, then it will take you 45 months to recover your closing-cost investment. In other words, you would "breakeven" after 45 payments.

Now, this would only make sense if you were absolutely certain that you planned to keep the loan for more than 5 years. Notice how I said "keep the loan" and did not say "keep the home." Even if you plan to keep the home for the rest of your life, if you are not 100% certain that you will not be refinancing again within the next 5 years, then please find a savings option like Example #2 and breakeven sooner.

Example #2: If you are able to select a refinance option that had a higher rate with a cost of $1000 but still saved you $70 per month, then you would breakeven after 15 payments. If you are certain that you will be in "the loan" for more than 2 years, then this is a great deal. Now, let's analyze how both of our examples compare after five and ten years. At the five-year mark (60 payments), Example #1 would have a net savings of $1500, while Example #2 would have a net savings of $3200. Pretty cool, huh?!? See how there are 2 price tags on every mortgage?

At the ten-year mark (120 payments), Example #1 would have a net savings of $7500, while Example #2 would have a net savings of $7400. So, it is at the ten-year mark that the "higher cost" loan passes the "higher rate" option. This is the type of simple analysis that you need to know, in order to put yourself into the best loan possible.

# Chapter 2: Remember there is also a cost to doing nothing!

It is pretty amazing when I come across people who have been deliberately overpaying on their home loans for more than a year or two. An entire year is a very long time to be overpaying $50 or more for anything. While many of us can justify paying $19.99 per month for a gym membership that we use sparingly throughout the year, we cannot and should not ever justify paying more on our homes than we already have to.

We cannot control the property taxes that we are going to pay, the utilities or the home insurance. Actually, we can control the two latter but that is another topic for another day. Let me start over.

While we cannot control the property taxes on our homes, we can prevent overpaying on our home loans. If I had a dollar for every time that I heard someone tell me that $50 was not enough savings to justify a $425 loan cost (which is the cost of an appraisal where I live), I would almost have my house paid off by now. For those of you doing the math on a $50/month savings with a $425 loan cost, that would be a 10-month breakeven point. Anything with less than a one year recovery period is an absolute no-brainer.

So, this person's cost for not refinancing, and doing nothing at all, would be $50 per month. If you add this to his/her monthly $19.99 gym membership, $200 cable bill and $300 fast food tab, then we are starting to recognize some of these people. Don't we?

# Chapter 3: But I don't want to restart another 30 years

This is one of the most popular reasons on why people do not refinance and it is truly a valid concern. If we all refinanced every few years, than we would never have our homes paid for. But we should always choose to pay less interest, if the costs can be recovered quickly enough. In other words, if we can breakeven in a timely fashion, we should always choose to pay less.

Let's take a look at an example to illustrate this. Four years ago, Mr. Johnson took out a 30-year loan for $160,000 at 4.625%. This had a monthly loan payment (ignoring property taxes and insurance) of $822.62 per month. Today, he has an opportunity to refinance into a new 30-year loan for $150,000 at 4.00%. This would generate a new monthly payment of $716.12, which could provide a much needed payment relief of $106/month for someone like Mr. Johnson, because he is barely getting by financially. (See Appendix 1a)

But for those fortunate people who do not need the payment relief (because they have good savings), they can simply take the new loan with a lower interest rate and continue to pay the "old" loan payment. So, if they continued to pay $822.62 on the new $150,000 loan at 4%, they would pay off the new loan in just under 23.5 years. Wow! That would take 2.5 years off of the twenty-six years remaining on the existing loan, which is almost $25,000 in interest savings! Remember, this huge savings came without increasing this person's monthly outgo. Again, this simply *maximized* this person's money.

# Chapter 4: VA and FHA loans are the easiest loans to refinance

Like anything in life, some things are going to be easier than others. When it comes to mortgage refinancing, VA and FHA loans are the easiest loans to refinance. I say this to help encourage people with these loans to jump a little quicker to exploring refinance opportunities. This fact should not discourage everybody else who still has a legitimate opportunity to improve their mortgage. Remember, what we learned in Chapter 2 and how there is still a cost to doing nothing.

The primary reason that VA and FHA loans are easiest loans to refinance is because they have a streamline options that does not require a new appraisal for the new loan. The appraisal is typically the only upfront cost of doing any new mortgage. When you can eliminate this upfront cost, then you can get a "free attempt" to improve your mortgage. You would have nothing to lose by applying, and everything to gain. On the other hand, when an appraisal is needed (which can cost $425 or more), you do run the risk that the home will not appraise for enough and lose this fee altogether.

Another reason why VA and FHA loans are easy to refinance is because they typically have better rates and lower refinance costs. Also, in many cases, these borrowers get to skip a house payment.

When refinancing other loans, many of these same benefits can be acknowledged if the appraisal comes in high enough. Besides regular qualification criteria, the appraisal can really make or break a deal. (See Appendix 1b) Remember the old saying, "you cannot steal 2nd base without taking your foot off of 1st base." A $425 gamble may save someone $25,000 or more! This would be a great "steal" of a deal. (See Appendix 1c)

# Chapter 5: What ever happened to the HARP loan?

If you are a radio listener, you have probably heard a popular online mortgage company keep on talking about how "you could be eligible for a special, limited-time government refinance program called HARP" and to call one of their specialists to see if you qualify. They neglect to tell people that this HARP program (Home Affordable Refinance Program) only applies to some Conventional loans that were taken out prior to May 31, 2009.

While HARP has helped over 3 million Americans since its inception in March 2009, it has become less relevant over the last couple of years. So, don't let the radio advertisements fool you into thinking it is something new. Always do your homework, which is what you are doing now with this book!

# Chapter 6: Be careful with online rates and online companies.

On that note, please be very careful with online companies that promise you the world. If it sounds too good to be true, then it usually is. Also, it is hard to hold a mortgage loan officer accountable when he/she is hundreds or thousands of miles away. When you are trying to improve the biggest financial obligation you may ever have in your lifetime, you should try to work with an individual that you can trust. Most online companies or toll-free numbers are call centers that pass you around whenever you call in. Not to mention, they make you feel like a transaction and not a person. Get the personal service that you deserve. (See Appendix 1d)

# Chapter 7: The 7 top reasons that people refinance their mortgages

- Better Rate
- Lower Payment
- Debt Consolidation
- Home Improvement
- College
- Reverse Mortgage
- Divorce/Death

Obviously, there can be many other reasons on why people refinance their home loans. If you have any questions on any of those listed above or if you have another scenario, feel free to email or call us anytime.

# Chapter 8: Pay it forward!

If you found this book helpful, please share it with others. There is nothing better than helping others. That is why I have been a Mortgage Loan Officer for over 18 years. I truly love helping people. It is an amazing honor and privilege when someone trusts me with his/her home loan. It is even more amazing when they feel that sense of relief every single month when they are paying their house payment. The relief that comes from knowing you are paying less than what you were and knowing that you are *maximizing* your money!

I hope that I have provided you with some valuable information and helped you become more confident with refinancing a home loan. Please feel free to share your thoughts, testimonies, ideas and/or questions with us at: MaximizeYOUReverything@gmail.com.

# Appendix 1: More Golden Nuggets to help guide you

a) It is very sad when I meet someone who didn't refinance when they would have had the chance (because they had a good paying job), only to apply when things got rough and now they no longer qualify to improve their mortgage situation. Please don't wait until it is too late. Refinance if it makes sense and while you can!

b) While it is impossible to know exactly what your home can appraise for, it is critical to have a general idea of what it could appraise for. Many people check their estimated home values at Zillow.com, while others call their real estate agent for a ballpark estimate. Still others have a great idea of what their home may be work by knowing what similar homes have been selling for, in recent months.

c) If you happen to have a low appraisal that is lower than what your property taxes are being assessed, you can give your Assessor's Office a copy of the appraisal and request that your property taxes be adjusted accordingly. It can't hurt to try.

d) It can be hard to find a knowledgeable and trustworthy loan professional with your mortgage needs. I think it is especially challenging when you feel you are working with a desperate salesperson who does not have your best interests in mind. To get around this, feel free to call or email us anytime. If my team is not licensed in your area, we will find you a loan officer that we would trust with our own friends and family.

# About The Author

Author, consultant, instructor and home mortgage expert Michael Baltazar specializes in helping homeowners reach their financial goals by empowering his clients with valuable and relevant information.

Even though he has a sales position within the mortgage industry, Michael does not consider himself to be a salesman. Instead, he considers himself to be a "helpsman" and strives to help as many people as possible.

If you are serious about improving your mortgage situation or if you are a mortgage professional in need of mentorship, feel free to visit Michael's website at MichaelBaltazar.com for more information or email us at: MaximizeYOUReverything@gmail.com.

We are happy to help!